Simple Ways to Make Teaching math More Fun

Bob Algozzine and James Ysseldyke

SOPRIS WEST EDUCATIONAL SERVICES
A CAMBIUM LEARNING COMPANY

BOSTON • NEW YORK • LONGMONT, CO

07   06   05   04   4   5   6   7

ISBN 1-57035-028-0

Illustrations by Tom Oling
Cover design by Londerville Design
Text layout and design by Sherri Rowe
Edited by Marjorie Raizman

Published and Distributed by

SOPRIS
WEST
EDUCATIONAL SERVICES

4093 Specialty Place • Longmont, CO 80504 • (303) 651-2829
www.sopriswest.com

50MATH/03-04

About The Authors

Bob Algozzine has been a teacher most of his adult life; the rest of the time he was a student. He loves math and playing with numbers. In his first class, he taught students with learning disabilities: Donnie and Phyllis were two real challenges. He was sort of a math genius and she hated math. Working with them started a lifelong search search for a "bag of tricks" to keep one step ahead of students like Donnie and Phyllis. In this book, he shares some of the tricks that make teaching math fun.

James Ysseldyke is a school psychologist and special educator. He has used his love of mathematics to teach professionals to use classroom assessments more effectively. In this book, he shares professionally tested interventions that are guaranteed to make teaching math fun.

Contents

Introduction
What This Book Will Do For You. 1

Chapter 1
Basic Training 3
  Take Them The Way They Are, But Expect
    Them To Change 4
  Do It To Them Before They Do It To You. . . . 4
  School Should Be A Place To Fail 4
  School Should Be Fun. 5
  Good Teaching Is Good Teaching 5

Chapter 2
Effective Planning Makes A Difference 9
  Make The Classroom A Part Of Your Plan . . . 9
  Try To Ask The Right Questions 10
  Try A New Instructional Routine 11

Chapter 3
Classroom Management Makes A Difference. . 15
  Use Rules To Manage Instruction 16
  Monitor Disruptions Systematically 19
  Handle Disruptions Efficiently 21
  Make Students Respond And Participate . . . 22

Chapter 4
Presenting Instruction Makes A Difference . . 25
  Create Open Worksheets 26
  Let BINGO Change Your Life. 33
  Use Palindromes To Practice Math. 39
  Practicing Math With Palindromes. 40
  A Few More Pretty Good Palindromes 41

Use Lotteries To Improve Attention
  And Skills 44
Have Multiple Assignments For Practice . . . 45
Teach Alternative Algorithms 47
Use Games To Increase Interest 54
Using Field Trips To Practice Math 58
Use Tricks And Teasers For Transitions 68
Integrate Language And Math Activities . . . 71
Find Some Transition Treasures 73
Use Problem-Solving To Improve
  Achievement 75

Chapter 5
  Evaluating Instruction Makes A Difference . . 81
  Check First, Ask Questions Later. 82
  Evaluate Frequently And Humanely 83
  Evaluate Frequently And Directly 85

I N T R O D U C T I O N

What This Book Will Do For You

Every teacher in school knew Armand. He was a "living legend" at Nosecone Elementary School. His reputation preceded him year after year in each new classroom. If "marches to a different drummer" was defined in the dictionary, Armand's picture could be used to illustrate it.

A day with Armand was like a bad week with most other students. The nature, frequency, and duration of his behavior were what made him tough-to-teach. Here's a typical sample of some of his "stuff":

1. Teacher asks a simple question: Who knows the answer to 2 + 2? Armand shouts out "six," while others with hands raised wait to be called.

2. Armand makes at least six trips to the pencil sharpener during independent seatwork. After 40 minutes, pencils have been destroyed and little work is done.

3. Five minute trips to the rest room usually last 30 minutes for Armand; he typically returns with an "escort."

4. Armand's parents can't control him. Nobody can control Armand.

5. Presenting a lesson with Armand in the class is a real challenge. If his teacher can manage to keep him from calling out answers for a short period of time, she usually has to deal with his constant comments of a "humorous" tone during the rest of the class period.

6. Armand's scores on academic achievement measures are dropping despite "above average ability."

Armand is a student who is tough-to-teach. And, while not every classroom has a student like Armand, every classroom has some kids who are tough-to-teach. Teaching these students makes teaching seem like a war. Teaching these students sometimes takes the fun out of teaching.

This book is about teaching math and making it fun. It's a practical book, full of useful ideas and tactics you can use immediately.

Enjoy! And remember one thing—teaching should be fun!

Top *10* Reasons Kids Hate Math

· · · · · · · · · · · · · · · · · · · ·

10. Numbers make them sick.

9. People who like math are really gross.

8. What good is math, anyway?

7. Familial Innumeracy Syndrome Habits (FISH).

6. Math *IS* their worst subject.

5. Too many right answers.

4. Grownups make them hate math.

3. They think there's only one way to get the right answer.

2. Somebody always gets the right answer before they do.

1. Nobody shows them that doing numbers can be fun!

CHAPTER

Basic Training

Most teachers have no problems identifying students who are tough-to-teach. Not completing assigned tasks, breaking rules, arguing, doing the opposite of what is requested, fighting, constantly seeking attention, lying, cheating, stealing, and being a general pain in the neck are among the widely respected characteristics of these students. Of course, few tough-to-teach kids display all of these problems, and sometimes their behavior is not considered a problem by all of their teachers.

In our work helping teachers with students who are tough-to-teach, we have found that spending time discussing characteristics seems to have a cathartic, mildly therapeutic effect. Teachers feel better when we listen to all the things a tough-to-teach kid does to drive them crazy, but, generally, simply listening doesn't do much to improve classroom instruction. Don't misunderstand our point. Identifying characteristics is important, but it doesn't point the way to what should be done. And worrying about or trying to change all those problems may just drive us crazier.

Instead of fixating on causes and characteristics, following are some fundamental beliefs that help us win the war against students who are tough-to-teach.

Take Them The Way They Are, But Expect Them To Change

Often teachers spend inordinate amounts of time trying to find out what's wrong with their students. The prevailing view is that knowing underlying causes leads the way to identifying cures. It works for a few, often serious problems, but generally not for the common, surface behaviors displayed by students who are simply tough-to-teach. And, more importantly, time spent searching for causes is not time spent working on cures or teaching.

Do It To Them Before They Do It To You

In working with students who are tough-to-teach, there is no substitute for planning and action. The most successful teachers of such students are those who achieve a simple goal: Stay one step ahead of them. This means knowing the enemy and having plans for the battle.

School Should Be A Place To Fail

In the game of "Twenty Questions," one player thinks of a person, place, or thing, and another player tries to guess it by asking questions that can be answered with "yes" or "no" responses.

I'm thinking of a number between 1 and 1000. What is it?

- Is it greater than 500? No.
- Is it less than 250? Yes.
- Is it less than 100? Yes.
- Is it less than 50? No.
- And so on.

It's a simple game that has infinite variations. It makes people think. It also illustrates an interesting fact.

In the game of Twenty Questions, yes/no answers are equally important. They both provide useful information, and they both help us solve a problem.

Too often, schools are structured around just getting the right answer. Getting things wrong is viewed as failure. In the game of Twenty Questions, "getting things wrong" (e.g., answering "No, it's not greater than 500.") is just as good as "getting things right" (e.g., "Yes, it's less than 250."). Working with students who are tough-to-teach is like this. It doesn't matter if what they are doing is always right as long as they learn from what they do wrong. School should be a place to make mistakes and learn from them. After all, schools are full of teachers and teachers are experts at correcting mistakes and helping students learn from them.

School Should Be Fun

Being a kid is tough. School should help with the process, not hinder it. School should be a place where natural interests in learning are supported. School should be fun. Life is too short for teachers to spend fussing and fighting with kids who are tough-to-teach or feeling like a teacher who can't teach them.

Good Teaching Is Good Teaching

Teaching is systematic presentation of content. All the things teachers do can be grouped into four broad categories: planning, managing, delivering, and evaluating instruction.

The first step in effective teaching is planning. By using knowledge of their students' current levels of functioning, effective teachers decide what to teach and how to teach it. They also communicate their expectations for performance to their students so "everybody is on the same page."

In teaching, the best made plans are sometimes sabotaged by the only people they are designed to help. Teaching would be easy if there were no students to mess up the plans. Effective teachers know this and anticipate how they will manage disruptions during their instruction. Rules, rewards and punishments, and other management methods are used to achieve an organized, productive, task-oriented learning environment in which time is used productively, transitions between activities are used effectively, and few interruptions disturb the flow of instruction.

Delivering instructions means presenting, monitoring, and adjusting lessons to meet the needs of all students. The overall goal of effective teachers is high rates of successful performance by their students. They monitor their instruction and provide feedback to keep their students actively involved. They also adjust instruction to meet the needs of all their students.

Effective teachers also evaluate their instruction by monitoring students' understanding and engaged time. They keep records of progress and share them regularly with students and their parents. These data gathered during instruction are the basis for a continuing effort to improve their instruction and plan appropriate follow-up lessons.

Whether they teach students who are severely and profoundly good or a group of students who are tough-to-teach, effective teachers plan, manage, deliver, and evaluate their instruction. The goal of effective teachers is high rates of successful performance in key academic areas.

In teaching math, effective teachers rely on proven tactics and practical materials to strengthen the achievement and motivation of their students. When doing this, successful teachers rely on a few tried-and-true methods that make learning fun. The remainder of this book is packed full of simple ways to teach math and make it more fun.

To implement these ideas, you don't have to make drastic changes in your current program. Any classroom program can be enriched and strengthened with the proven tactics in this book. Our goal is to provide highly practical methods of helping you improve math instruction for students who are tough-to-teach.

And now, on with the show!

JUST *for* FUN

· · · · · · · · · · · · · · · · · · · ·

Try some wrong way addition:

```
  34     Add up or down the tens column and then continue adding
  12     up or down the ones column until you run out of numbers
  21     and reach the final sum (78) .
+ 11
  78     ┌─────────────────────────────────────────────────────┐
         │ 30+10=40+20=60+10=70+4=74+2=76+1=77+1=78             │
         └─────────────────────────────────────────────────────┘
```

Try these for practice:

```
  34              52
  26              27
  12              11
+ 21            + 16
     (93)             (106)
```

CHAPTER

Effective Planning Makes A Difference

Make The Classroom A Part Of Your Plan

Many teachers complain about the process of teaching math. Some complain that they have to spend so much time going over homework that they often have no time left to introduce new objectives or content. Others find that their assignments are so difficult for the majority of their students that they spend the instructional day reteaching rather than teaching. Most complain that they know very little about the progress of individual students until a test is given. And almost all math teachers believe that the class period is never long enough.

Planning can help. For example, using the classroom space effectively can give you a big advantage. U-shaped desk arrangements are more effective because students' written work can be checked more easily and quickly than in traditional arrangements. It also helps reduce problems in the back rows and back corners, making all students more a part of the instructional group. Isolation and "fooling around" are clearly more difficult in a U-shaped arrangement.

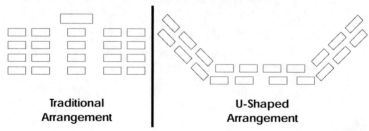

Traditional Arrangement	**U-Shaped Arrangement**

U-shaped arrangements also make it easier for students to work together in pairs or small groups.

Try To Ask The Right Questions

For many students, school goes like this: The teacher calls on somebody in the class. If that student gives the right answer, the teacher goes on to somebody else or continues teaching. If the student gives the wrong answer, the teacher calls on another student until the right answer is given. Often, if the right answer doesn't surface quickly, the teacher will answer the question and make a poignant remark about the quality of the current crop of students. The whole process is very frustrating for teachers and often provides incredible opportunities for some kids to make teaching tougher.

Asking the right questions can go a long way to improving the overall classroom environment. Effective teachers have a plan for using their questions. Here are some tips on using questions:

1. Try to wait after asking any question. Wait-time (i.e., the time between a question and response) has been shown to be related to the quantity and quality of student responses in many different content areas. Waiting at least three seconds, and sometimes longer than five, will bring amazing results. Also, this helps you avoid answering your own questions.

2. Try to avoid asking questions that require a simple yes/no response. Answers to this type of question tell little about what the student knows. After all, no knowledge has a 50-50 chance of being counted as correct.

3. Try to avoid using a student's name and signaling his question ("Jim, what's the sum of 4578

and 3459?"). Other students tend not to listen to the question if they know it is directed to a particular student. It also helps to avoid calling on a student immediately after asking a question ("What's the sum of 4578 and 3459, Jim?"). The secret is to ask the question and pause before nailing someone to answer it.

4. Try not to label the degree of difficulty of the question. Think about it:

    •   "Here's an easy one. What's a fractal?"

    If you know the answer, you don't take much satisfaction in it, since it was so easy. And if you don't know the answer, you're in worse shape.

5. Try to use question-answer instructional sessions sparingly. If students could learn mathematics from a lecture presentation, tape recorders would have replaced teachers long ago. Try to keep math instructional sessions more active and engaging. It will make a real difference.

Try A New Instructional Routine

Having a daily plan helps you get the most out of your math instructional time. It also helps in managing students who are tough-to-teach because the structure works in your favor. Here's an approach that works (see the Math Planning Guide on page 14):

1. Have an objective for the students to accomplish each day.

2. Have an activity that will help you gain control in the first five minutes of the class. Brain-teasers, math puzzles, and other simple math games work well.

3. Have a general strategy for homework correc-
    tion. But, maybe more importantly, limit home-
    work correction time to about ten minutes.
    Following are some approaches that will help:

    a. Write the answers on a transparency
        and let the class correct their own
        work.

    b. Have homework monitors
        responsible for correcting
        assignments use answer
        keys.

    c. Write the
        answers on
        the board and
        have students
        correct their
        own papers or a
        classmate's.

    d. Have the homework
        monitor read the correct answers from the an-
        swer key as students correct a classmate's paper.

    e. Have a plan for handling student questions.
        Have students place a tally mark on a chart to
        show which problems they would like to see
        solved, or select most frequently missed
        problems after homework has been corrected
        and solve them.

4. Have a plan for teaching new content and vary
    the ways you do it each day. A simple model is
    very effective and allows for considerable
    day-to-day variation. First, show the students
    what they are expected to do. This demonstra-
    tion illustrates how to get the right answer.
    Next, have students do a couple of problems and
    check their work. The purpose here is to have a

chance to check for errors and provide immediate, corrective feedback if needed. Then, have students practice on their own while you circulate among them to provide supportive and corrective feedback.

Vary the ways you have students work during independent practice. Finally, include a check/review period in which levels of mastery, problem areas, and general understanding are evaluated.

5. Have a homework or independent assignment ready before the class begins. This helps focus the teaching time and reduces the likelihood of some kids escaping without the assignment.

6. Have an activity ready for the last five minutes of class. This might include additional practice or review, as well as a preview of things to come. Use this time to build confidence, reinforce the day's experiences, and establish the importance of what you and the students have done.

Math Planning Guide

Date _____   Time _____   Class _____

1. Math objective(s) we are working on at this time

2. First five minutes (try to involve all students as quickly as possible)

3. Homework correction plan (transparency, board, student key)

4. Instructional plan (questioning, cues, practice, feedback, engagement)

5. Homework assignment (transparency, board, homework buddies)

6. Last five minutes (transition with a sense of purpose and accomplishment)

7. Special considerations (error correction, build on success)

CHAPTER

Classroom Management Makes A Difference

Discipline is consistently identified as a concern on public and professional opinion polls about education. Clearly, classroom disruptions are among the greatest deterrents to effective instruction noted by most teachers. Few of us are comfortable in situations that are unstructured and chaotic; this is particularly true for classrooms. Most students need and function better in orderly environments. This is why management and strategies related to it are part of effective teaching, especially with students who are tough-to-teach.

Effective classroom management involves preparing effective instruction. By doing this, effective teachers establish classroom rules and communicate them early in the school year. They teach students the consequences of following and not following their rules, and they handle rule infractions and other classroom disruptions as quickly as possible after they occur. An overriding concern for many effective teachers is having students manage their own behaviors.

Effective classroom management involves using time effectively. This means establishing routines and procedures, organizing physical space, setting transitions between work sessions, maintaining an academic focus, allocating time to academic activities, pacing instruction appropriately, and giving clear task directions.

Effective classroom management also involves establishing a positive classroom atmosphere. Students are more motivated to learn when teachers accept individual differences, interact positively, and create supportive, co-operative classrooms. Most kids like school more when teachers are accepting and caring. An overriding goal in classrooms of effective teachers is active student response; when managing instruction, effective teachers use a variety of tactics to accomplish this goal.

Use Rules To Manage Instruction

A characteristic of an effective school is orderly class-room climates. Effective teachers know that rules help them achieve and maintain order in their classrooms. They also know that children deal with rules differently at different ages. For example, younger children (kinder-garten through second grade) are more compliant and interested in pleasing their teachers than older students. Teachers of young children generally need to spend for-mal instructional time teaching rules and expectations as well as classroom procedures and routines.

Third to fifth graders have generally learned basic school rules (if early grade teachers were successful) and need help remaining focused on obeying the rules and pleasing teachers and others in authority. For these students, more time spent with rules, pro-cedures, and routines early in the year means less time with cuing, reminding, and teach-ing rules later.

Students entering adolescence are less eager to please teachers and more eager to please peers. Many resent rules and think questioning authority is "the right thing to do." The teacher's task becomes motivation-oriented and many times involves students, especially students who are tough-to-teach, in decision-making. This can be a very productive and useful component of a management plan.

Regardless of the student's age, some of them generally need consistent, formal instruction related to classroom and school rules. Here are some general tips for using rules effectively to help manage instruction.

- **Keep Rules Short And Sweet**

    Classroom rules are a must to achieve a good working classroom atmosphere. However, having too many rules can overwhelm students. Keep your classroom list of rules brief, making sure students understand exactly what is expected of them. Try to arrange the rules so the first letters of key words help students remember them. For example:

What We Do In School
Walk in the halls. Wait for the teacher. Display good behavior with peers. Show Interest in our work. Share positive comments.

- **Limit Number Of Rules**

    Limit the number of rules developed for a classroom to three to five. Having too many rules can weaken their impact since students will not be able to remember or focus on a large number. Rules should be general enough to cover a variety of classroom situations. More specifically, situations such as what to do during writing-center time can be addressed by developing procedures (steps for organizing and implementing specific activities) rather than by creating rules.

- **Post Rules To Minimize Misunderstandings**

  After identifying appropriate, reasonable rules, effective teachers generally post them in a conspicuous place in the classroom. They also frequently review the rules as a part of daily "business" at the beginning of the school day. It sometimes helps to separate school rules (e.g., No running in halls) from classroom rules (e.g., Ask permission to leave room).

- **Signal Rule Infractions To Prevent Misbehavior**

  Many teachers give warnings (e.g., raised eyebrow/evil-eye reminders) to students suggesting that they are "on the borderline" of misbehavior. Others simply ask students to repeat the rules when their behavior approaches noncompliance. Still others rehearse appropriate behavior as a method of preventing problems. For example, before leaving the room to go to a school assembly, one teacher asked her students to describe appropriate behaviors for traveling from their classroom to the auditorium and how they should act during the group activity. She also let them know the consequences for rule violations.

- **Display Rules On Chart**

  Display classroom rules on a chart in a highly visible area of the classroom. This will enable you to refer to the chart frequently for review or reminders. It will also encourage consistency in implementing rules since they will always be visible to both students and teacher.

- **Review Rules Regularly**

  Classroom rules should be reviewed periodically. Frequent reviews are essential at the beginning of the school year when rules are being established. Other times requiring review are immediately after vacation periods, prior to changes in routines or schedules, or during times when rule-breaking seems to be increasing.

Monitor Disruptions Systematically

Often, minor disruptions can be effectively managed by having students keep track of them. First, define the problem behavior in clear, understandable terms (e.g., tapping pencil or pen on desk, paper, or other surface to produce noise). Place a small chart on the target student's desk and have him or her note occurrences of the behavior on the chart. Often, the simple act of keeping track is sufficient to cause students to reduce levels of disruptive behavior (see example below):

Pencil Tapping (11/8 Through 11/12)
M //// //// //// ////
T //// //// ///
W //// ////
Th ////
F ///

Lotteries provide another way to monitor student disruptions. Start by giving each student a predetermined number of tickets with his or her name written on each one. Place the tickets in an envelope on your desk or the desk of each student. When a rule is broken or an inappropriate behavior displayed, remove a ticket from the student's envelope.

At the end of the day, collect all remaining tickets and place them in a lottery box. Select three or four tickets from the box and award prizes for good behavior to the winners. Even those students who are tough-to-teach quickly realize that their chances of winning are better when they have more tickets at the end of the day (when good behavior pays off).

Some teachers form classroom behavior teams (e.g., students sitting in the same row, class divided into thirds), give the teams a set of tickets, and remove tickets when a team member misbehaves. Others place a "wild card" in the lottery box, so any student or team will have a chance to win, even if overall performance for a day has not been outstanding.

Some teachers find it better to monitor appropriate behavior rather than call attention to inappropriate behavior. Management cards, lotteries, and group lotteries are easily modified to address this concern.

Hand Raising (11/8 Through 11/12)		
M	//// ////	
T	//// //// ///	
W	//// //// ////	
Th	//// /	
F	//// //// ////	

The key here is focusing on behavior. Try to catch students "being good" and provide rewards and recognition for it, but don't be afraid to monitor disruptive behavior as well (just don't make *it* pay off).

Handle Disruptions Efficiently

Nothing interferes more with effective instruction than disruptions created by some kids. Talking out of turn, joking, teasing, not being prepared, engaging in irrelevant activities, and generally disturbing the universe are among daily battles that must be fought with these students. Effective teachers handle disruptions efficiently.

- **Avoid Over-verbalizing**

  Over-verbalizing about an act of misbehavior tends to call attention to the problem and reinforce it—a result that is contrary to the desired outcome of eliminating it. When misbehaviors occur, verbalizations should offer either a solution or a negative consequence (e.g., "Pick up the crayons, now." or "Five minutes of time-out.") and nothing more. If it is necessary to explore the reasons for misbehavior, it is better done after a negative consequence has been delivered. Moralizing or nagging is not an appropriate follow-up for misbehavior.

- **Use Nondisruptive Techniques To Control Behavior**

  Minor misbehavior and misbehaviors that are just beginning can often be effectively controlled with nondisruptive techniques such as eye contact, proximity (move near the student's desk), or signals (pointing, shaking head, etc.). You must decide whether your attention might reinforce rather than eliminate the misbehavior by using these strategies. Such strategies are most effective when they can be used with one student without calling the attention of other students to the misbehavior.

- **Offer Choices to Avoid Power Struggles**

  Sometimes dealing with misbehavior results in a confrontation may be more disruptive. Such battles can be averted by offering choices. For example, if a student tends to resist accepting a consequence such as going to time-out, the student can be given the following choices: (1) Go to time-out now for five minutes, or (2) Go to time-out when you feel like it and spend 20 minutes, and have a letter sent to your parents.

These choices should be delivered in a calm, matter-of-fact tone and should be followed with the statement, "I hope you make a good decision." At this point, you should become involved with

students who are engaging in positive behaviors and ignore the misbehaving student until a compliance decision is made. Such choice presentations allow the teacher to withdraw immediately from a potential power struggle.

Make Students Respond And Participate

Effective teachers recognize the importance of productive, engaged time during instruction. They know they must manage their classrooms to be successful with all children. They use a variety of techniques to achieve this goal.

- **Change Positions To Control Engaged Time**

    A teacher's position can have positive effects on student behaviors. Sometimes inappropriate behaviors (e.g., not completing an assignment) can be modified simply by moving closer to a student.

- **Use Signals To Focus Attention**

  Students sometimes engage in behaviors without realizing they are interfering with productive classroom activities. Effective teachers use cues and signals to let these students know that their behavior is inappropriate. Sometimes a raised voice brings attention to problem behavior; some teachers turn off the classroom lights to "suggest" that their group is too noisy.

  A special education teacher uses verbal cues to redirect behaviors. During a lesson on dinosaurs, one of her students started tapping a pen on the edge of his desk. At an opportune moment, the teacher gained the student's attention with a "psst" and an eye glance at the pen. The student stopped tapping the pen and continued with his work.

- **Use Lotteries To Keep Students Actively Engaged**

  Identify several behaviors that reduce the likelihood that students will start assignments and stay actively engaged with them (e.g., making comments about appropriateness of work, not starting on time). Write target behaviors on tickets (see below) and have students put them in a lottery box on the teacher's desk each time an appropriate response is exhibited. Periodically select a lottery winner from the tickets that have been entered during the day.

Lottery Ticket Example

(front of ticket)

Providence Day School Lottery Ticket 9/9

(back of ticket)

Started work within 10 seconds of assignments Name: _____

CHAPTER

Presenting Instruction Makes A Difference

Effective teachers recognize the importance of maximizing time spent on academic response and minimizing the time spent on transition activities that do not result in active academic response. Sounds like a simple idea and it is. The problem is sticking to it with a few tough-to-teach kids around. A simple "trip" to the pencil sharpener or other diversionary tactic can easily and quickly cause a class to start late or a well-planned classroom presentation to be side-tracked.

Having classroom materials and aids organized and ready before beginning an instructional presentation is a sure-fire way to minimize transition time and maximize instructional time. It also helps to practice closing activities and opening others. Because effective teachers recognize the importance of engaged time, they reward students who use transition time effectively.

Other teachers use transition time to introduce subsequent activities and motivate students to look forward to them. They also establish clear procedures for transition periods. Quiet talking, bathroom breaks, or free movement around the classroom are acceptable transition activities. They spend time telling students what is allowed and what is expected, and they spend time teaching them how to quickly refocus for instructional periods that follow transitions.

Effective teachers also ensure that every student responds at some point during a lesson. Some keep track of individual responses by having students mark index cards attached to their desks each time they answer an instructional question. When students are doing independent seatwork, these teachers circulate among them and ask for explanations of what they are doing. They try to keep their classrooms active so nobody sits very long without engaging in successful academic response.

The key to effective teaching is maximizing academic learning time. This chapter contains successful ways of accomplishing this goal.

Create Open Worksheets

When you find a good idea, you should abuse it. A favorite of some teachers is to create worksheets that can be used with different skills. For example, one teacher created "Pick A Pear," which was a picture of a tree with blank pears drawn on it. Math facts or problems, word problems, math definitions, or any other information that students need to practice are written on the pears.

Students who are tough-to-teach enjoy choosing their work from an open worksheet rather than having it assigned in a traditional form. Ideas for other open worksheets can be taken from students. Always consider their interest level when putting one together (e.g., jumping ramps with skateboards, putting tires on cars (or taking them off), catching fish, buying clothes).

Students who are tough-to-teach also like creating their own worksheets. The examples on the following pages illustrate computation exercises that are easily modified to provide practice at different levels of skill development.

Have students complete the prepared sheet and then have them make up their own by using the open sheet format.

Directions:

Circle ten sets of three numbers that add up to eight. You must use all the numbers in the puzzle, but you can circle each number only once. When circling numbers, you may not cross another line.

2	0	8	0	1
1	5	4	7	0
3	1	3	5	1
4	1	1	5	2
7	0	0	2	0
1	8	0	7	1

Directions:

Circle any three numbers in a row that add up to 22. The numbers must be vertical, horizontal, or diagonal. You can circle some numbers more than once. How many sets can you find?

7	9	6	8	3	7	1	4
5	6	3	7	5	4	2	9
4	9	9	7	6	9	5	9
1	8	2	5	7	9	3	2
9	1	6	8	8	1	4	7
4	7	6	9	9	5	8	5
6	7	9	8	1	7	2	8
9	8	5	7	7	1	8	9

Directions:

Go down the ladder for each of the three numbers. The answers at the bottom should be the same.

Try starting with different numbers.

	7	5	9
1. Add 3	(10)	(8)	(12)
2. Multiply by 2			
3. Subtract 4			
4. Divide by 2			
5. Subtract original number			

	6	20	200
1. Add next number	(13)	(41)	(401)
2. Add 9			
3. Divide by 2			
4. Subtract original number			

	6	20	13
1. Add 3	(9)	(23)	(16)
2. Multiply by 2			
3. Subtract 4			
4. Divide by 2			
5. Subtract original number			

Directions:

Using number tiles, rearrange numbers so six sets of three each add up to 17.

Have a friend try it.

Try it with a different target number.

11	12	1
10		2
9	17	3
8		4
7	6	5

- -

(solution)

2	12	3
6		10
9	17	4
7		8
1	11	5

Amazing Work

Directions:

Work through the maze from the upper-left to the lower-right, passing through only those boxes where four enclosed numbers add up to 13. You may proceed up, down, left, or right, but not diagonally.

9121	7054	9031	5602	7222	1842	6530	3281	4432	1165	0832
7321	5062	3028	9060	5371	0760	3622	4612	5800	1833	1138
5332	8701	1813	1940	2605	9040	1494	2243	3343	6501	8041
6341	2065	2722	2325	1048	6063	2803	1309	2722	4424	2155
1910	6133	1191	6710	4513	3033	1570	1941	0614	1363	8200
4081	3820	5252	1561	3901	9303	0652	4234	5152	6313	3037
7210	0517	0618	1048	2514	1273	6211	7802	9002	1721	4252
9220	8050	2191	7411	1823	6701	5530	4144	4045	2119	9013
7501	5352	7011	4345	0508	8113	1822	6014	9005	8114	3602
0661	4713	8401	5126	5323	1724	6237	9024	2812	0481	2902
8032	3712	2632	7311	0706	4720	1075	6016	3145	2406	1219

Amazing Work

Directions:

Pick a number (e.g., 13). Create a maze by placing numbers in boxes so that the path of the maze follows boxes containing numbers that add up to the target number. Proceed up, down, left, or right, but not diagonally.

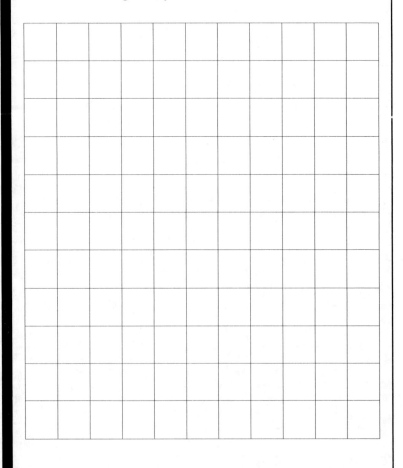

Let BINGO Change Your Life

Motivating students to practice basic math facts can be a tough assignment. Reinforcing independent study skills is important, but often difficult to do. Rewarding successful practice of the behaviors necessary for effective peer relations is not easy. Providing an environment in which students practice important social behaviors (e.g., controlling negative overreaction, controlling disruptiveness, and effective listening) is a noteworthy goal that is often overlooked because other goals take up time first. You can use BINGO to address all these goals.

This is what you need: flash card facts or similar stimulus response content, BINGO boards, markers, a scorecard, a list of rules, players, a caller, a recorder, and a scorekeeper.

- **Here's How To Play BINGO:**

  Students clear their desks except for BINGO cards and game rules. Markers are distributed. The caller indicates to the recorder the fact he or she is about to target (e.g., 9), then reads the word equation twice: "Five plus four equals _____." Students cover the appropriate answer

with a marker. Play continues until the first student raises his or her hand and calls "BINGO."

The responsibility of the caller is to indicate each fact targeted to the recorder, then read each number equation loudly and clearly. The responsibility of the recorder is to write down each fact targeted. When students raise their hands and call "BINGO," the recorder checks each answer they have covered to make sure they have not made an error. If they have made an error, play continues. If they have a BINGO, academic points are written down by the scorekeeper, boards are cleared, and a new game begins.

Each student calling BINGO must have five items covered horizontally, vertically, or diagonally unless the teacher has stated that a different format will be used. No student is declared a winner unless the recorder has checked his or her numbers.

As play proceeds, the teacher circulates around the room, rewarding students for appropriate behavior. The teacher specifies this behavior by writing down points earned next to the behavior written on the rule sheet. For each winner, the scorekeeper writes down the number of points previously agreed that winning students will earn.

At the end of the game independent seatwork is given to students. As students complete their work, the teacher calls them to her desk and records behavior points earned. Then the class as a whole watches as each student moves his or her chart piece up the "ladder of success" (an academic point chart).

Sample game rules, an implementation schedule, and game cards follow.

- **Here Are Some Game Rules You Can Use:**
  1. All students must remain seated during the game.
  2. All students must remain silent during play.
  3. Students must keep their eyes on their own BINGO boards.
  4. When a student has covered five words horizontally, vertically, or diagonally, he or she must raise a hand and say "BINGO."
  5. No winner will be declared until the recorder has checked all facts.
  6. During checking periods, no student can put a marker on a number.

- **Job Responsibilities Include:**
  1. The caller is to indicate each fact targeted to the recorder, then read each word equation loudly and clearly.
  2. The recorder is to write down each number targeted and check any student who has called "BINGO."
  3. The scorekeeper is to record academic points for winners.

- **Sample Implementation Schedule:**
  Monday:
    - Teacher distributes content (e.g., new math facts) for week
    - Teacher teaches facts and answers students' questions
    - Students study words for homework
  Tuesday:
    - Students peer tutor in pairs
    - Teacher circulates, reinforcing appropriate behavior

> – Teacher orally quizzes students, reinforcing correct answers

Wednesday:

> – Students prepare BINGO sheet using targeted facts
>
> – Teacher rewards appropriate behavior
>
> – Students study math facts for homework

Thursday:

> – Students peer tutor in pairs
>
> – Students take written test on math facts
>
> – Teacher corrects and records test grades

Friday:

> – Students and teacher play BINGO
>
> – Teacher rewards appropriate behavior
>
> – Teacher awards points to winners

Facts We Are Practicing This Week

1. 18 - 7 = _____
2. 15 - 4 = _____
3. 11 + 6 = _____
4. 17 - 9 = _____
5. 12 - 3 = _____
6. 5 + 7 = _____
7. 16 - 7 = _____
8. 14 - 8 = _____
9. 9+8 = _____
10. 13 - 6 = _____
11. 12 - 4 = _____
12. 6 + 7 = _____
13. 11 - 5 = _____
14. 18 - 6 = _____
15. 4 + 6 = _____
16. 18 - 9 = _____
17. 12 - 6 = _____
18. 7+7 = _____
19. 17 - 7 = _____
20. 18 - 0 = _____
21. 8+6 = _____
22. 17 - 5 = _____
23. 16 - 9 = _____
24. 9+8 = _____
25. 15 - 9 = _____
26. 12 - 5 = _____
27. 9+6 = _____
28. 17 - 4 = _____
29. 16 - 6 = _____
30. 9 + 9 = _____

BINGO card set up by student
after practicing facts

B	I	N	G	O
9	7	15	11	13
10	8	12	14	6
6	7	FREE	8	9
10	11	12	13	14
17	18	10	18	17

Blank BINGO card suitable for copying and mass distribution.

B	I	N	G	O
		FREE		

Use Palindromes To Practice Math

Some children love numbers. They like the way they can be arranged to make interesting sequences. They like the way their meaning is constant. They like the way people use them to create and solve problems.

Many students hate numbers and doing math. They seem to dread having to practice number facts, solve math problems, and use math in any way. Some of it comes from adults they hang around with. Think of the times you've heard adults brag about "not being good at math."

A palindrome is a word, phrase, sentence, or number that is the same when written forward or backward. The name Bob is a palindrome. "Pot top" is a palindrome. The number "4334" is a palindrome. In math, palindromes can be produced by repeatedly adding numbers in a prescribed sequence. Here's how it goes.

Take any two numbers ⟶ 23 and 45

Add them together ⟶
$$\begin{array}{r} 23 \\ +45 \\ \hline \end{array}$$

Stop if the sum is a palindrome, ⟶
otherwise **reverse the sum**
$$\begin{array}{r} 68 \\ +86 \\ \hline \end{array}$$

and **add** them together **again.** ⟶
$$\begin{array}{r} 154 \\ +451 \\ \hline \end{array}$$

Continue this process **until the**
$$\begin{array}{r} 605 \\ +506 \\ \hline \end{array}$$

sum is a palindrome. ⟶ 1111

The mathematical principle here is not important. Most kids are generally intrigued by the way "it always works out," and some of them take it as their mission to prove it won't always work. Many math haters will work for hours finding sets of palindromes (e.g., solve in five steps with answer being 1111) that you can use on their classmates. Some examples are presented on the following pages.

Practicing Math With Palindromes

Many kids love to do math palindromes and group them based on their characteristics (e.g., set with final sums and same number, sets that solve in more than five, ten, or 20 steps). Here are examples of some they have found:

23	31	82	17	47
+45	+78	+13	+92	+21
all ones in four steps	all ones in three steps	all ones in four steps	all ones in three steps	all ones in four steps
20	41	99	23	24
+66	+18	+10	+36	+62
all ones in four steps	all ones in four steps	all ones in three steps	all ones in four steps	all ones in four steps
65	793	479	551	80
+90	+430	+128	+582	+75
all fours in four steps	all fours in two steps	all fours in three steps	all fours in two steps	all fours in four steps
92	99	87	67	68
+65	+57	+99	+89	+89
all eights in four steps	all sixes in four steps	sixes and nines in four steps	all sixes in four steps	all eights in four steps

These solve in more than four steps.

34	87	24	98	52
+63	+95	+45	+84	+45

A Few More Pretty Good Palindromes

These solve in eight or more steps.

746	347	461	736	582
+140	+242	+227	+658	+304

These solve in more than 12 steps.

516	291	391	532	537
+383	+382	+906	+239	+343

These solve in more than 20 steps (trust us).

332	478	833	515	527
+646	+213	+932	+176	+451

79	34	75	25	26
+19	+55	+12	+64	+72

93	926	427	103	13
+94	+551	+156	+865	+85

A Palindrome Project

Start with the number 1, reverse it (1), and add it to the starting number (1). If answer is palindrome, stop, otherwise continue until the number is a palindrome. Do it for all numbers between 1 and 99.

1	2	3	4	5	6	7	8	9
+1	+2	+3	+4	+5	+6	+7	+8	+9
2	4	6	8	10	12	14	16	18
				+01	+21	+41	+61	+81
				11	33	55	77	99

No.	Steps	Palindrome	No.	Steps	Palindrome	No.	Steps	Palindrome
10	1	11	40	1	44	70	1	77
11	1	22	41	1	55	71	1	88
12	1	33	42	1	66	72	1	99
13	1	44	43	1	77	73	2	121
14	1	55	44	1	88	74	1	121
15	1	66	45	1	99	75	2	363
16	1	77	46	2	121	76	2	484
17	1	88	47	1	121	77	3	1111
18	1	99	48	2	363	78	4	4884
19	2	121	49	2	484	79	6	44044
20	1	22	50	1	55	80	1	88
21	1	33	51	1	66	81	1	99
22	1	44	52	1	77	82	2	121
23	1	55	53	1	88	83	1	121
24	1	66	54	1	99	84	2	363
25	1	77	55	2	121	85	2	484
26	1	88	56	1	121	86	3	1111
27	1	99	57	2	363	87	4	4884
28	2	121	58	2	484	88	6	44044
29	1	121	59	3	1111	(89)	24	8813200023188
30	1	33	60	1	66	90	1	99
31	1	44	61	1	77	91	2	121
32	1	55	62	1	88	92	1	121
33	1	66	63	1	99	93	2	363
34	1	77	64	2	121	94	2	484
35	1	88	65	1	121	95	3	1111
36	1	99	66	2	363	96	4	4884
37	2	121	67	2	484	97	6	44044
38	1	121	68	3	1111	(98)	24	8813200023188
39	2	363	69	4	4884	99	6	79497

A Nightmare On Palindrome Street

Beware of 89 and 98. They will eventually solve as a palindrome, but clearly they require patience, persistence, and mathematical power.

```
      89                    85189247
     +98                   +74298158
     187                   159487405
    +781                  +504784951
     968                   664272356
    +869                  +653272466
    1837                  1317544822
   +7381                 +2284457131
    9218                  3602001953
   +8129                 +3591002063
   17347                  7193004016
  +74371                 +6104003917
   91718                 13297007933
  +81719                +33970079231
  173437                 47267087164
 +734371                +46178076274
  907808                 93445163438
 +808709                +83436154439
 1716517                176881317877
+7156171               +778713188671
 8872688                955594506548
+8862788               +845605495559
17735476               1801200002107
+67453771              +7012000021081
85189247               8813200023188
```

Use Lotteries To Improve Attention And Skills

Lotteries are sometimes promoted as a means of providing funding for the educational system in a state. Teachers often support them because they have seen the powerful effects of lotteries on their students. They use them several ways:

Some teachers have students take tests and quizzes on small slips of paper instead of the traditional 8 1/2" x 11" sheet. After each item is administered, the teacher collects them and puts them in a lottery drawing box for later use.

Periodically during the day, the class holds a lottery drawing. If the name, date, and information on the ticket is correct, the entrant wins a prize or elects to reenter the super lottery held at the end of the week.

There are numerous variations on this theme. Math problems, math facts, social studies facts, main ideas of reading passages, current events, and other academic content information can be practiced using lotteries. Classroom behaviors also work:

- "Anyone currently sitting down gets a lottery ticket."
- "Thank you for bringing in a pencil today. Here's a lottery ticket for you."

Here are some math examples:

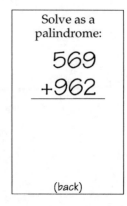

Name	Solve as a palindrome:
_____	569
Date	$+962$
_____	
(front)	(back)

```
┌─────────────────────────┐     ┌─────────────────────────┐
│ Name                    │     │ Bill had two            │
│ ─────────────────────   │     │ dozen yoyos.            │
│                         │     │ He sold one-            │
│ Date                    │     │ third of them           │
│                         │     │ for $1 each. He         │
│ ─────────────────────   │     │ sold the rest for       │
│           (front)       │     │ $1.50 each.             │
└─────────────────────────┘     │ How much did            │
                                 │ he make in all?         │
                                 │                         │
                                 │           (back)        │
                                 └─────────────────────────┘
```

Have Multiple Assignments For Practice

I taught middle-school-aged boys in several states. I was always amazed by how much they claimed to know or be able to do and how little they often actually could do. Most of them needed to practice simple academic skills like basic math facts regularly (the school psychologist always told me so). Typically, when I would present a worksheet like Exhibit A to them, I'd hear the standard lament: "I ain't doing that again, it's baby stuff."

Now I figured I always had a few choices. I could give them a "voice volcano" (jump up real close to their faces and shout "**DO IT!**" as loud as I could), or I could send them to the principal for insubordination training, or I could fight some other war to get the work done. Or, I could use the more subtle, "Gosh, I'm sorry. Gee, you are right." approach. That's what I did.

If they didn't like a sheet like Exhibit A (see page 46), I'd make a big deal about how right they were and how I should be more careful in what I assign. I'd rummage through some files and come up with one that looked like Exhibit B. If that was accepted, the battle was over. If not, Exhibit C was offered in negotiation (e.g., "Try a few of these."). By carefully constructing the worksheets, I was able to disguise the obvious fact that it was basically the same stuff.

Never failed to amaze me how dumb they thought the enemy was or how sweet the smell and feel of victory could be.

Exhibit A

2 +2	3 +3	4 +4	5 +3	6 +1	3 +6	2 +5	6 +3
2 +4	5 +3	5 +4	5 +2	3 +1	3 +4	2 +6	1 +4

Exhibit B

234 +234	536 +316	264 +531	725 +243
555 +434	332 +214	143 +645	353 +246

Exhibit C

234563 +234316	264725 +531243	555332 +434214	143353 +645246
224562 +234216	165723 +431243	452332 +435217	453352 +145346

Exhibit D (only for the truly intractable)

234563264725 +234316531243	555332143353 +434214645246
224562165723 +234216431243	452332453352 +435217145346

Teach Alternative Algorithms

An algorithm is a systematic step-by-step procedure used to solve a problem or find an answer. The most common written algorithm for addition involves two procedures: adding single digits using basic fact knowledge and carrying, regrouping, or exchanging when appropriate to reach a final solution. It looks like this:

$$\begin{array}{r} \text{⑪} \\ 573 \\ +\ 297 \\ \hline 870 \end{array}$$

Students who are tough-to-teach sometimes don't appreciate the simplicity and joy to be derived from putting this algorithm into practice. Many of them do appreciate alternative algorithms (different ways to arrive at the same solution to a problem).

$$573 + 297 = 500 + 200 + 70 + 90 + 3 + 7 = 870$$

Step-by-step solutions, lattice solutions, left-right methods, tens methods, and two-times methods are alternative algorithms that sometimes capture the interest of students who are tough-to-teach. Here's how they go:

Step-By-Step Addition I

```
 584
+397
```
11	Sum of ones
170	Sum of tens
800	Sum of 100s
981	Final sum (sum of sums)

Step-By-Step Addition II

```
 584
+397
```
11	Sum of column one
17	Sum of column two
8	Sum of column three
981	Final sum (sum of sums)

Lattice Work

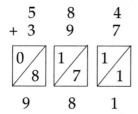

Left-Right Methods

To add 343 and 156, first add the 100s (300 + 100), then the tens (40 + 50), then the ones (6 + 3) to obtain 499. Alternatively, think:

$$300 + 100 = 400 + 40 + 50 = 490 + 6 + 3 = 499.$$

and

$$3 \times 123 = 3 \times 100 + 2 \times 30 + 3 \times 3 = 369.$$

Doing Tens Subtraction

Here's an algorithm where students only need to know addition and subtraction facts from ten to solve more complex problems:

$$
\begin{array}{r}
②\,⑩\\
327\\
-\,183\\
\hline
144
\end{array}
$$

RULE: Subtract if you can (7 - 3). When you can't (2 - 8), put a ⑩ above the column and drop the number next to it (3) by one ②. Subtract (10 - 8) and add the remaining number in the column (2). Finish by following the rule (2 - 1).

$$
\begin{array}{r}
⑤\,⑩\\
②\,⑩\\
631\\
-\,498\\
\hline
133
\end{array}
$$

RULE: Subtract if you can. When you can't (1 - 8), put a ⑩ above the column and drop the number next to it (3) by one ②. Subtract (10 - 8) and add the remaining number in the column (1). Finish by following the rule (subtract if you can). When you can't, (2 - 9), put a ⑩ above the column and drop the number next to it (6) by one ⑤. Subtract (10 - 9) and add the remaining number in the column (2). Finish by following the rule (5 - 4).

$$\begin{array}{r} \text{⑦⑩} \\ \text{①⑩} \\ 820 \\ -\ 298 \\ \hline 522 \end{array}$$

RULE: Subtract if you can. When you can't (0 - 8), put a ⑩ above the column and drop the number next to it (2) by one ①. Subtract (10 - 8) and add the remaining number in the column (0). Finish by following the rule (subtract if you can). When you can't (1 - 9), put a ⑩ above the column and drop the number next to it (8) by one ⑦. Subtract (10 - 9) and add the remaining number in the column ①. Finish by following the rule (7 - 2).

Drop Zeros Multiplying

$$\begin{array}{r} 34 \\ \times\ 12 \\ \hline 8 \\ 60 \\ 40 \\ 300 \\ \hline 408 \end{array}$$

    8   2 x 4
  60 2 x 3 and drop a 0
  40 1 x 4 and drop a 0
300 1 x 3 and drop two 0s
408 Add 'em up.

$$\begin{array}{r} 857 \\ \times\ \ \ 9 \\ \hline 63 \\ 450 \\ 7200 \\ \hline 7713 \end{array}$$

   63 9 x 7
 450 9 x 5 and drop a 0
7200 9 x 8 and drop two 0s
7713 Add 'em up.

Two Times Multiplying

```
   34
 x 12
   68
```
Think 2 x 34

```
  340
  408
```
Think 10 x 34
Add 'em up.

```
   62
 x 24
  248
```
Think 4 x 62

```
 1240
 1488
```
Think 20 x 62
Add 'em up.

Doin' Them "Guzintas"

Find the quotient and remainder for 5739 ÷ 31 (31 "guzinta" 5739 how many times?).

```
 31)5739     How many 31s in 5739?
  - 3100      Guess: 100
    2639      How many 31s in 2639?
  - 1550      Guess: 50
    1089      How many 31s in 1089?
  -  930      Guess: 30
     159      How many 31s in 159?
  -  155      Guess: 5
       4
```

Add up your separate guesses: 100
50
30
5

Answer: 185 r 4

Six "guzinta" 3584 how many times?

```
        1
        6
       90
      500
   6/3584    How many 6s in 3500?
   - 3000    Guess: 500
      584    How many 6s in 580?
   -  540    Guess: 90
       44    How many 6s in  40?
   -   36    Guess: 6
        8    How many 6s in 8?
   -    6    Guess: 1
        2
```

Answer: 597 r 2

More Lattice Work

Multiply to fill squares.

Add down diagonals.

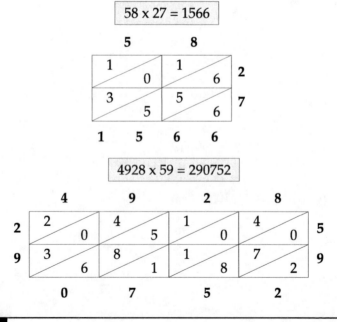

$58 \times 27 = 1566$

$4928 \times 59 = 290752$

Use These For 2 x 2 Lattice Work

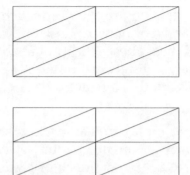

Use These For 2 x 3 Lattice Work

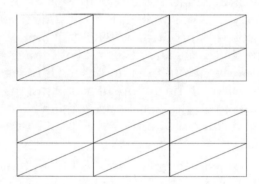

Use These For 2 x 4 Lattice Work

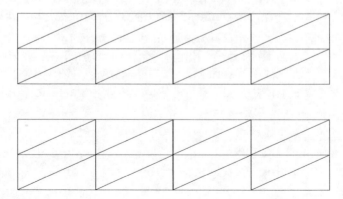

Use Games To Increase Interest

Many students who are tough-to-teach have a natural affinity for decks of playing cards (homemade or commercial) and dice. These readily available materials can be used to play a variety of simple games that make students practice math. Here are some examples:

- **"Tensky"**

    This is a simple card game where students practice basic facts. You need four sets of index cards numbered 1–9 (or a deck of cards with tens and face cards removed and aces serving as ones).

    Each player receives four cards. The remaining cards are placed face down in a stack among the players. A player begins by putting down any two cards that produce a "tensky" (sum of 10). He or she then asks any other player for a card that can be added to one of his or her cards to make another "tensky." If the opponent has any of the requested cards (e.g., 4), he or she gives them all to the player. If the student doesn't have any, he or she tells the player to "take a hike."

    The player then takes a card from the remaining stack and continues with his or her turn if the card matches the requested card. If it doesn't match, another player has a turn. Whenever a "tensky" is found, it is placed face up in front of the player.

    Players who run out of cards may take two more from the stack. Play continues until all cards are paired as "tenskies." The winner is the one with the most pairs. ("Twelvesky" is a variation played using cards 2–10.)

- **Value War**

    To play this game, students need a deck of ordinary playing cards (face cards can be removed, if you want them to use numbers only). Divide the cards evenly, face down, among all players (extra cards are given to the winner of the first "battle"). Have the players prepare their "armies" by placing their cards in a pile without looking at them.

Battles are waged by having players turn over top cards simultaneously. Battles are won by determining who is the "general" with the strongest "soldier" (highest value card). Spoils of war (turned over cards) are collected by the winning general.

If there is a tie, the generals involved place three cards face down and turn over the fourth. The winner is determined by the highest value card. If a tie occurs again, the same procedure is followed until a winner is declared.

When a general has used the first army, his spoils of war pile is shuffled and used as reserves. Play continues until one player has all the cards or until a preset time limit has passed.

- **Concentration**

  Start with four sets of index cards numbered 1–9 (or a deck of cards with tens and face cards removed, and aces serving as ones). Place the cards in a 6 x 6 design face down on a table. Have a player turn over any two cards. If the sum is 10, the player picks up the cards and takes another turn. If the sum is not 10, the cards are shown to other players and replaced in their former positions.

  Play continues until all cards have been picked up as pairs that sum to 10. Simplify the game by using half the cards or vary it by using cards 2–10 for sums of 12.

- **Math War**

  Start with four sets of index cards numbered 1–9 (or a deck of cards with tens and face cards removed

and aces serving as ones). Deal all cards out evenly face down to each player; any cards left over are taken by the first winner. Each player selects two soldiers (turns over two cards) to represent him in battle, adds their values together, and announces their "total power." The highest sum wins the battle and takes all soldiers that are in play.

If there is a tie, the generals involved select two more soldiers, calculate their value, and determine total power again. Play continues until all the soldiers have been won or until a preset time limit has expired. Each time a stack of cards has been used, newly acquired cards are reshuffled and battles continue. Once a general is out of soldiers, the game is over.

Math war can be varied by adding soldiers to battles (e.g., sum of top three cards) or by varying the mathematical operation used to determine winners (e.g., subtraction or multiplication rather than addition).

- **"Sumsky"**

  Start with four sets of index cards numbered 1–9 (or a deck of cards with tens and face cards removed and aces serving as ones). Shuffle cards and have them face down in a pile. Players take turns drawing cards and trying to make a sum of 10 with other cards that have been turned up (any combination of cards can be used). If 10 cannot be summed, the card is left face up. Any time a 10 is summed, the player picks up all the cards and makes a "book." The player with the most books wins. The game can be played with other sums (e.g., 15, 18, 20), and students can keep track of books by using simple graphs and other forms of data recording.

- **"Hilo"**

  Start with four sets of index cards numbered 1–9 (or a deck of cards with tens and face cards removed and aces serving as ones). Shuffle the deck and have each player draw two cards, form a two-digit number using them, and place it face down. Players then indicate whether their number is "Hi" (largest two-digit number) or "Lo" (smallest two-digit number) among those that have been formed.

  Player(s) predicting Hi reveal their numbers before players predicting Lo. Each player must read the number correctly to receive a point. An additional point is awarded for a correct prediction, and the game stops after a preset total number of points has been reached. The game can be varied by using three cards or four cards.

- **"Sumtotal"**

  Start with deck of cards, face cards counting zero and aces serving as ones). Deal five cards to each player. First player checks cards for sum of 33. If he or she has it, one point is awarded and all cards are returned to deck and shuffled for a new hand. If the student doesn't have it, he or she draws a card from the remaining deck, then places a card in a discard pile.

  Play continues with players drawing from top of either pile of cards. The first player to place five cards down with a total of 33 wins the hand and receives a point. Ten points wins a game (unless a preset time limit was set). The game can be varied by changing the "sumtotal" (e.g., 37 or 29) and/or allowing players to use other math operations when totaling five cards (e.g., $33 = 4 \times 8 + 3 / 3 + 0$).

- **Triple Digit**

  Start with four sets of index cards numbered 1–9 (or a deck of cards with tens and face cards removed, and aces serving as ones). Shuffle the deck and have each player draw two cards. First player draws an additional card and places it or another card face up in the center of the table. Next player draws a card, adds a card to the pile, and announces the sum. Play continues with each player drawing, adding cards, and declaring the sum of all cards that have been discarded. Play can be varied by having one (e.g., tens) added **or** subtracted (tens can be subtracted) and declaring the first person to go over 100 as the loser.

Using Field Trips To Practice Math

A field trip is an experience designed to add to ongoing instructional programs. Most of the time, field trips are elaborate, well-planned visits to businesses, museums, or other places away from school. Most children enjoy them because they provide opportunities to learn in different environments and chances to practice what's being learned by applying it in the real world.

In-class field trips can serve the same purposes. For example, math field trips can provide experiences searching for specific information in reference books or the library. They can also provide opportunities for students to make estimates and find data to support them, or they can be used simply to provide practice using numbers to answer questions.

Field trips can also be used as homework for parents to use on vacations, at restaurants, on shopping trips, or during other family activities.

Answers can be located from a set of choices (e.g., set of number tiles) or written directly on the field-trip sheet (see the examples following). Some teachers laminate the sheets so they can be used by different students. Others place them in manilla folders at a Math Learning Center.

Field Trip (Example)
Using Numbers Between 1–9

Answer: | Find the number that is the same as quintuplets.

Answer: | Find the number of white stripes on the American flag.

Answer: | Find the number of legs on an octopus.

Answer: | Find the number of days in a week.

Answer: | Find the number of sides in a triangle.

Notes:

Field Trip
Stuff Around The Room

Answer: [ ] Find three objects with numbers greater than 50 on them.

Answer: [ ] Find three round objects.

Answer: [ ] Find three cylinders.

Answer: [ ] Find three triangles.

Answer: [ ] Find three different objects that have the same size and shape.

Notes:

Field Trip
Stuff Around The Room

Answer: [ ] Find three decimal numbers.

Answer: [ ] Find a rectangle, square, triangle, and circle that are the same color.

Answer: [ ] Find a rectangle bigger than the sheet this field trip is printed on.

Answer: [ ] Find the smallest rectangle in the room.

Answer: [ ] Find a rectangle with width greater than height.

Notes:

Field Trip
Calendars

Answer:

Find a month with a Tuesday date that is a perfect square.

Answer:

Find the month with the week with the highest total for the dates of seven days added together.

Answer:

Find a month where only one Saturday is a multiple of five.

Answer:

Find sum of all Saturdays in a month that has five Sundays.

Answer:

Find product of second and third Sundays in a month where products of first two Saturdays is more than 75.

Notes:

Field Trip
Calendars

Answer:

Find a month with the week with the lowest total for the dates of seven days added together.

Answer:

Find three dates in a row whose sum is a multiple of 11.

Answer:

Find a month where two Saturdays are a multiple of three.

Answer:

Find product of last two Mondays in a month where the products of first two Mondays is less than ten.

Answer:

Find product of last two Wednesdays in a month where the product of first two Wednesdays is more than 29.

Notes:

Field Trip
Telephone Book

Answer:

Find a telephone number with the sum of all digits greater than 30.

Answer:

Find a telephone number that contains four perfect squares.

Answer:

Find two telephone numbers whose difference in the last four digits is less than 100.

Answer:

Find a telephone number in the Cs with digits that have a sum greater than the number before and after it.

Answer:

Find a telephone number with digits that have a sum less than 20.

Notes:

Field Trip
Telephone Book

Answer:

Find a telephone number that is a multiple of eight.

Answer:

Find a telephone number that is a multiple of five.

Answer:

Find two telephone numbers whose sum of the last four digits is greater than 8000.

Answer:

Find a telephone number in the Vs with digits that have a sum less than the number before and after it.

Answer:

Find a telephone number with digits that have a sum greater than 40.

Notes:

Field Trip
Grocery Advertisement

Answer: | Find an item costing more than 45¢ but less than 89¢.

Answer: | Find three items that cost less than $1.00.

Answer: | Find five items whose cost would be exactly $3.69.

Answer: | Find an item that costs an amount that is a multiple of five.

Answer: | Find two items with the smallest difference between their prices.

Notes:

Field Trip
Grocery Advertisement

Answer: | Find two items whose prices are reversed (e.g., 69¢ and 96¢).

Answer: | Find three items whose total cost is less than $1.00

Answer: | Find three items of different prices that are all palindromes.

Answer: | Find an item with a price that is a three-digit palindrome.

Answer: | Find the price of the most expensive coffee in a can.

Notes:

Field Trip
TV Guide

Answer: | Find a palindrome with at least two digits.

Answer: | Find the largest four-digit number between pages 7-15.

Answer: | Find a movie time between 90 minutes and two hours.

Answer: | Find a movie time longer than two hours.

Answer: | Find the sum of the highest even-number TV channel and the highest odd-number TV channel.

Notes:

Field Trip
TV Guide

Answer: | Find a sports program with a team from our state.

Answer: | Find the sports program with the earliest broadcast time.

Answer: | Find the sports program with the latest broadcast time.

Answer: | Find six numbers that are not used to indicate TV channels.

Answer: | Find a decimal number or a number indicating dollars and cents.

Notes:

Field Trip
Mail Order Catalogs

Answer: | Find four different items that cost the same amount.

Answer: | Find three different items whose sum is greater than $100.

Answer: | Find the item that costs the most and the item that costs the least.

Answer: | Find two items whose difference in price is $20.

Answer: | Find an item that costs twice as much as another item.

Notes:

Field Trip
Mail Order Catalogs

Answer: | Find the cost of something that you pay for in measured units (e.g., $4.00 per pound or $1.29 per yard).

Answer: | Find an item that would cost less than $100 if you bought ten.

Answer: | Find two items whose sum is greater than $150 and whose difference is less than $30.

Answer: | Find seven different items whose total cost is between $300 and $350.

Answer: | Find three of the same type of item (e.g., sweaters) and find the difference between the highest and lowest costs.

Notes:

Field Trip
Measurement

Answer: Find something about a yard long.

Answer: Find something about one foot long.

Answer: Find something between six and nine inches long.

Answer: Find something containing one pint of liquid.

Answer: Find something containing at least two cups of a gas.

Notes:

Field Trip
Measurement

Answer: Find something four centimeters high.

Answer: Find something 13 centimeters long.

Answer: Find something weighing about one kilogram.

Answer: Find something containing at least one liter of fluid.

Answer: Find something greater than two meters in height and greater than ten kilograms in weight.

Notes:

Field Trip

Answer:

Answer:

Answer:

Answer:

Answer:

Notes:

Field Trip

Answer:

Answer:

Answer:

Answer:

Answer:

Notes:

Use Tricks and Teasers for Transitions

Students who are tough-to-teach love to play games. Some of them are even tempted to be interested in math games. For example: Think of a number; add 10; multiply by 4; add 200; divide by 4; subtract original number. Is the answer 60? Here are some more:

- Select any number greater than 100 and multiply it by 9. Select one of the digits of this result as the "missing digit." Find the sum of the remaining digits. Continue adding digits in resulting sums until you have a one-digit number. Subtract that number from 9. Is that the missing digit? If not, try again with another number. Determine which missing digits this procedure will find.

- Select any four-digit number. Arrange the digits to form the largest possible number and the smallest possible number. Subtract the smallest number from the largest number. Use the digits in the difference and start the process over. Keep repeating it. What happens?

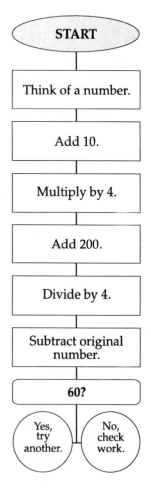

Solving problems like these requires doing the same math many kids love to resist. Putting them in flowcharts makes math fun.

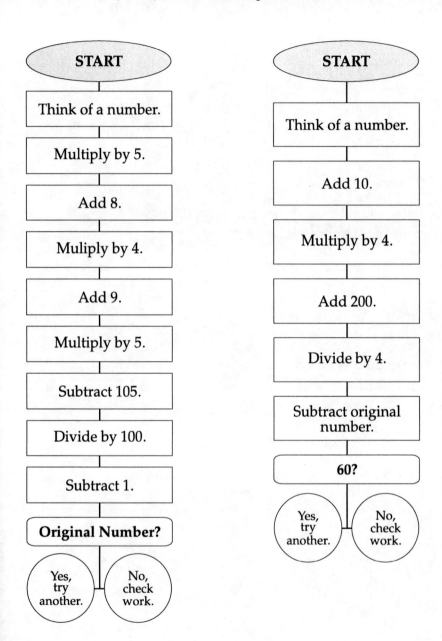

START

Think of a number.

Multiply by 5.

Add 8.

Muliply by 4.

Add 9.

Multiply by 5.

Subtract 105.

Divide by 100.

Subtract 1.

Original Number?

Yes, try another.

No, check work.

START

Think of a number.

Add 10.

Multiply by 4.

Add 200.

Divide by 4.

Subtract original number.

60?

Yes, try another.

No, check work.

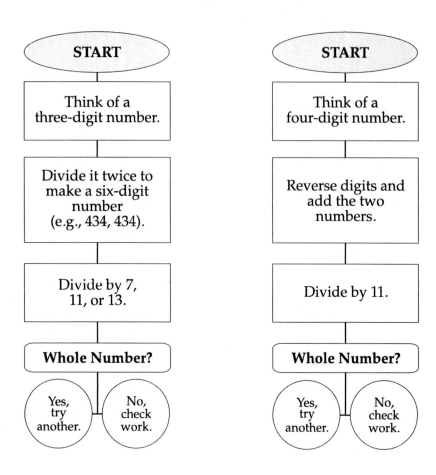

START

Think of a
three-digit number.

Divide it twice to
make a six-digit
number
(e.g., 434, 434).

Divide by 7,
11, or 13.

Whole Number?

Yes,
try
another.

No,
check
work.

START

Think of a
four-digit number.

Reverse digits and
add the two
numbers.

Divide by 11.

Whole Number?

Yes,
try
another.

No,
check
work.

Integrate Language and Math Activities

In the book, *My Father's Dragon*, by Ruth Stiles Gannett, a little boy packs his knapsack to leave home. During his trip, he uses some of the things he packed. The story provides an excellent opportunity for an addition and subtraction activity. Students can calculate how many things are in the knapsack at the beginning of the trip, then keep running totals as the trip progresses and items are used.

Activities:

- Read the story to the students and have them take notes as items are included in the knapsack.
- Read the story and have the students keep track of the number of items included in the knapsack.
- Create packing lists (see page 72) and have the students complete them as if they were making the trip. Add trip logs (see page 72) and have the students complete them (specifying amounts when unspecified) as if they took the trip.
- Have the students create their own packing lists and/or trip logs and share them with a friend from another grade.

My Father's Dragon Packing List	
	What? How much? How many? Amount?
1. Chewing gum	_____
2. Lollipops	_____
3. Rubber bands	_____
4. A compass	_____
5. A toothbrush	_____
6. Toothpaste	_____
7. Magnifying glass	_____
8. A sharp jackknife	_____
9. A comb	_____
10. Fruit	_____
11. Hair ribbons	_____
12. Clean clothes	_____
13. Food for the trip	_____
14. Food for the trip	_____
15. Books	_____
Total Number of Items	_____

My Father's Dragon Trip Log	
Started with _____ items.	
	How many left?
1. Used one rubber band	_____
2. Ate some food	_____
3. Found a bag of oranges	_____
4. Ate three oranges	_____
5. Ate one piece of gum	_____
6. Lost magnifying glass	_____
7. Lost knife and comb	_____
8. Ate some fruit	_____
9. Tied ribbons on trees	_____
10. Gave two books away	_____
11. Found six rubber bands	_____
12. Ate some food	_____
13. Read a book	_____
14. Gave toothbrush away	_____
15. Gave a lollipop away	_____
Number of Items Left	_____

Find Some Transition Treasures

Transitions or the times between activities are prime times for some kids to find wonderful things to do. Many teachers use simple activities to fill transition times. Here are some treasures they use.

- **Pattern Block Pictures**

    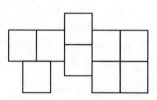

    Have students select a pattern block from laminated construction paper forms or actual blocks in a variety of geometric shapes (square, trapezoid, parallelogram, triangle, hexagon, or rhombus) and create a picture with it.

    Have students write at least three directions to use in coloring the picture (e.g., color five red, color three green, and one yellow or color 5/9 red, 3/9 blue, and 1/9 white).

    Duplicate the pictures, place them in folders, and have them ready for students to complete during transitions.

- **Dart Boards**

    Draw a dart board target on the chalkboard. Give students three "darts" (chances to hit the target). Have them list all the scores that are possible if all three "darts" hit the target. Change the numbers to vary the game. Prepare some targets on paper and have the students place numbers on them before throwing their "darts."

    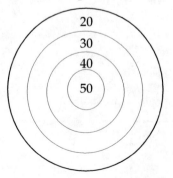

- ## Charge, Charge, Charge

Prepare some sheets with credit balances and have students go shopping to spend their money (see the example).

Charge, Charge, Charge	
Credit Balance	$2.00
Bubble Gum 25¢	$1.75
Book 95¢	.80
Candy 25¢	.55
Bubble Gum 25¢	.30
Final Balance	$ .30

Charge, Charge, Charge

CREDIT BALANCE						

Purchases	Cost	Amount Left
Bubble Gum		
Magic Trick		
Comics		
Ice Cream Bar		
Pencils		
Notebook		
T-Shirt		
Candy Bar		
Apple		
Baseball Cards		
FINAL BALANCE		

Use Problem-Solving To Improve Achievement

The importance of problem-solving has been stressed in every report addressing education reform. A key recommendation for improving problem-solving skills in mathematics follows:

Teach for understanding by providing hands-on experiences with real-life problems that stress exploration and encourage curiosity.

What do traditional problem-solving activities look like? Here are a few examples:

1. Alea had 22 balloons. If she gave four balloons to each of five friends, how many balloons would she have?

2. Joel had $2.46. His sister gave him $4.00. If he wanted to by a CD for $13.00, how much more money would he need?

3. Greg hit a baseball 250 feet. Scott hit one 180 feet. How much farther was Greg's hit?

4. At 6:00 A.M., the temperature was 42°. By noon the temperature had risen 19°, but the wind chill was -17° and four boys had colds. What time is it in Hong Kong?

There are exciting alternatives that help make problem-solving fun. Here's an example.

Have two students work together using the matrix following. Taking turns, one student (playing as "O") selects a problem for the other student (playing as "X") to answer. If the right answer is provided, an X is awarded. If a wrong answer is provided, an O is awarded. The game continues until one player has three Xs or Os in a row. As illustrated on the following pages, the problem content can be varied to accommodate differing levels of math instruction.

Xs or Os

How many days until Christmas?	Make five triangles using ten toothpicks.	The answer is 36. What is the question?
What three even numbers add up to 54?	Make a number story with these numbers: 18, 29, 11.	Find three things exactly eight inches long.
How many weeks in two years?	Make 50¢ using seven coins.	Find the largest number on the front page of a newspaper.

Xs or Os

Use a calculator to find the sum of the digits in your phone number.	How many days until your next birthday?	Draw a picture using only rectangles, triangles, and circles.
Count the number of days until school is out.	Find all the ways you can make 25¢.	Write a story about 7 + 5.
Think of a question for all students in the class to answer. Ask the question. Make a graph of results.	If you have four coins, how much money could you have?	Gather ten objects. How many ways can you sort them?

Pick One—Any One

Number of times the minute hand passes 12 during 24 hours.	An outfit is on sale for 30% off. You pay $40. What was the original price?	Cost of tickets to rock concert for the whole class.
Height of flagpole in front of school.	What time will it be 1000 hours from now?	Storage space needed for collection of 200 CDs.
Amount of wallpaper needed to cover walls in principal's office.	Cost of gas for school buses in school system for one week.	Draw two squares using only five lines.

FIELD WORK
(Problems Requiring Math Solutions)

Directions:

Prepare a set of 5 x 8 index cards with "field work" problems on one side. Have students select a card and complete some problem-solving tasks. First, have them decide if more information is needed to estimate an answer to the question. Next, have them develop a method for arriving at the correct answer, and then actually find an answer using their method. Finally, have them compare answers with other students, illustrate the variability on a graph, and make up field work to exchange for additional practice.

How many bricks are on the outside structure of the school building?

Do you need more information? _____ What? _____

What's your prediction? _____

How could you come up with the right answer?

_____

_____

_____

_____

What's your answer? _____

Compare and share methods and answers, then make "field work" for a friend to complete.

FIELD WORK
(Problems Requiring Math Solutions)

How many shoes have laces?

How close can you get to a bird?

How many names are in the White Pages of your phone book?

How many pieces of popcorn would fill a file cabinet?

How many people have blond hair?

How many people live in brick houses?

How many people drive white cars?

How many people have fall birthdays?

How many teachers are over 40 years old?

How much money in four meters worth of dimes?

How many golf balls will fill a suitcase?

How much storage space is needed for a collection of 200 CDs?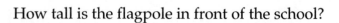

How much does gas for school buses cost in one week?

How tall is the flagpole in front of the school?

How many words on the front page of today's newspaper?

CHAPTER

Evaluating Instruction Makes A Difference

Evaluation is an important part of teaching. It is the process by which teachers decide whether the approach they are using is effective with an individual student. Teachers also use evaluation to decide whether their methods and materials are effective. And evaluation data are used to make important decisions like whether to refer students to specialists, whether to change interventions, and whether (or when) to exit students from programs.

Formative evaluation occurs during the process of instruction: The teacher collects data during instruction and uses those data to make instructional decisions. Summative evaluation occurs at the end of instruction, when the teacher administers a test to determine whether a pupil has met instructional objectives.

Principles of evaluation instruction include: monitoring students' understanding, monitoring engaged time, maintaining records of students' progress, informing students of progress, using data to make decisions, and making judgments about students' performance.

Students must understand what teachers expect them to do in the classroom, which means teachers must monitor the extent to which students understand directions. Effective teachers do more than simply ask a student: "Do you understand what I want you to do?" It is too easy for students simply to respond "yes" without actually having any idea of what they are expected to do. Effective teachers ask students to show them or tell them what they are going to do, then observe the students' responses. Teachers monitor success rate in deciding whether or not students understand what it is they are to do. A low success rate may mean simply that students do not understand what they are to do.

Ideas for how to monitor instruction with students who are tough-to-teach follow.

Check First, Ask Questions Later

Some things you never forget. For us this was the time an intern described observing a "problem student" in a Virginia Beach elementary school. It changed our views about independent practice, seatwork, and learning problems. What struck us as unusual was the intensity with which the student was completing portions of her assignment and the consistency with which she was getting the answers wrong. The intern had the student do five problems and then checked them. The student had everything wrong. When we looked at her work, this is what we saw:

$$
\begin{array}{ccc}
34 & 54 & 67 \\
+66 & +87 & +59 \\
\hline
910 & 1311 & 1116
\end{array}
\quad \text{and so on.}
$$

Now, we admit the answers were wrong. But there was no excuse for somebody not teaching the student how to do the problems right. Everybody makes mistakes; smart people learn from them. In our opinion, there is no more serious error than having students practice errors on independent practice or homework assignments.

After that experience, we vowed never to let a student do more than three problems without checking them and reteaching the content if our evaluation revealed that the student had not learned the proper solution sequence. When students work on independent assignments in math, spelling, or other basic skill areas, effective teachers try to check the first answer students produce to ensure that they'll be ahead of the "error practicing monster."

Regardless of whether they are right or wrong, many teachers ask their students about the solution. They try to verify that the answer was not a fluke, if it was correct. They use an incorrect answer as an indication that reteaching is in order. When they notice errors, they return to those students more frequently than others just to be sure the error practicing monster doesn't return. They find that a little time checking answers up front pays huge dividends by reducing questions that have to be asked later. Clearly, an ounce of evaluation early prevents a pound of remedial cure later.

Evaluate Frequently And Humanely

Keeping track of student performance and progress is a time-consuming, but important, activity. Effective teachers are vigilant. They continuously scan the classroom to spot students who are not actively engaged, and they take steps to engage students who are not participating.

- **Use Activities To Showcase Student Skills**

    Some teachers use activities to point out positive qualities of students. For example, a fourth grade teacher selects a different student each day to be "teacher" and make important decisions (e.g., time for recess) after consulting with other adults in the room. The teacher also periodically singles out a different student to be "king/queen for a day" and receive special rewards. She has classmates write positive comments about the student being treated as royalty, and she incorporates some of them into a letter that is sent home with the student at the end of the school day.

Another teacher puts pictures of her students on a bulletin board and periodically provides lists of positive characteristics for each of them. She also lets classmates contribute comments to the "VIP BULLETIN BOARD."

- **Be Flexible In Difficult Situations**

   Sometimes assignments or daily activities will generate considerable frustration for students. Making changes reduces frustration and keeps interactions positive. For example, if a spelling test is going to be timed for the first time, careful selection of words (mostly easy ones) can help reduce the problems created by the timing.

   When spontaneous factors interfere with ongoing activities, effective teachers change their plans to prevent frustration and negative consequences. Many of them keep notebooks with "great ideas for tough times" to use when regular plans need to be adjusted.

- **Help Students See Their Strengths**

   Give students a chance to select their favorite activities to do sometime during each school day. Usually, they will select things they do well, and performances on these activities are an excellent source of information for improving students' opinions about themselves and their school experiences.

Evaluate Frequently And Directly

The latest research in evaluation indicates that direct and frequent measurement is the best foundation for an effective monitoring plan. Ongoing, continuous monitoring of student progress is a component of effective programs in general and special education. Teachers using direct and frequent measurement principles are concerned with three primary questions: What should be measured? How frequently should it be measured? How should obtained information be used?

Behaviors directly linked to progress in the ongoing curriculum are the best targets for instructional evaluation activities. The greater the match between content being taught and content being tested, the more useful the instructional evaluation. The purpose here is to decide what a student has mastered or not mastered in the content being taught so that instruction can be modified to make a difference on any subsequent evaluations.

If students are learning subtraction facts for numbers less than 20, direct and frequent measurement of their progress should be completed for subtraction facts for numbers less than 20. A daily timing of the number of problems completed in one minute can be a very effective evaluation activity (see page 87). First, it provides frequent feedback on a curriculum-based goal and provides useful information on specific problem areas (e.g., 12 - 9 does not equal 4) that can be corrected quickly. It also provides a measure that can be used frequently.

Ideally, curriculum-based evaluation should occur on a daily basis; at least once a week is more common and much easier to accomplish. One teacher we have worked with used one-minute daily timings as a basis for deciding what math content should be taught, remediated, or reviewed. She prepared 30-item samples like those on page 87 and administered them to students every day for the duration of the subtraction unit.

Student performance on direct and frequent measures should be used to provide feedback and illustrate progress. Preparing simple graphs of daily performance helps many teachers monitor their students' progress. Copy the Math Performance Recording Chart (see page 88) and use it to keep track of your students' direct and frequent progress in math.

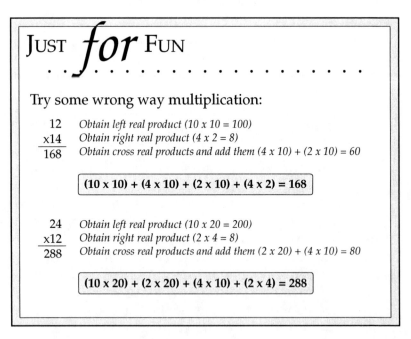

JUST *for* FUN

Try some wrong way multiplication:

$$
\begin{array}{r}
12 \\
\times 14 \\
\hline
168
\end{array}
$$

Obtain left real product (10 x 10 = 100)
Obtain right real product (4 x 2 = 8)
Obtain cross real products and add them (4 x 10) + (2 x 10) = 60

(10 x 10) + (4 x 10) + (2 x 10) + (4 x 2) = 168

$$
\begin{array}{r}
24 \\
\times 12 \\
\hline
288
\end{array}
$$

Obtain left real product (10 x 20 = 200)
Obtain right real product (2 x 4 = 8)
Obtain cross real products and add them (2 x 20) + (4 x 10) = 80

(10 x 20) + (2 x 20) + (4 x 10) + (2 x 4) = 288

Hope you enjoyed the trip.

Subtraction Timing

1. 18 - 7 = _____
2. 15 - 4 = _____
3. 11 + 6 = _____
4. 17 - 9 = _____
5. 12 - 3 = _____
6. 5 + 7 = _____
7. 16 - 7 = _____
8. 14 - 8 = _____
9. 9 + 6 = _____
10. 13 - 8 = _____
11. 12 - 4 = _____
12. 6 + 7 = _____
13. 11 - 5 = _____
14. 18 - 6 = _____
15. 4 + 7 = _____
16. 18 - 9 = _____
17. 12 - 7 = _____
18. 7 + 5 = _____
19. 17 - 5 = _____
20. 18 - 8 = _____
21. 8 + 5 = _____
22. 17 - 5 = _____
23. 16 - 9 = _____
24. 9 + 8 = _____
25. 15 - 8 = _____
26. 12 - 5 = _____
27. 9 + 7 = _____
28. 17 - 4 = _____
29. 16 - 4 = _____
30. 8 + 6 = _____

Name: _____
Date: _____
Time: _____

Subtraction Timing

1. 18 - 7 = _____
2. 15 - 4 = _____
3. 11 + 6 = _____
4. 17 - 9 = _____
5. 12 - 3 = _____
6. 5 + 7 = _____
7. 16 - 7 = _____
8. 14 - 8 = _____
9. 9 + 6 = _____
10. 13 - 8 = _____
11. 12 - 4 = _____
12. 6 + 7 = _____
13. 11 - 5 = _____
14. 18 - 6 = _____
15. 4 + 7 = _____
16. 18 - 9 = _____
17. 12 - 7 = _____
18. 7 + 5 = _____
19. 17 - 5 = _____
20. 18 - 8 = _____
21. 8 + 5 = _____
22. 17 - 5 = _____
23. 16 - 9 = _____
24. 9 + 8 = _____
25. 15 - 8 = _____
26. 12 - 5 = _____
27. 9 + 7 = _____
28. 17 - 4 = _____
29. 16 - 4 = _____
30. 8 + 6 = _____

Name: _____
Date: _____
Time: _____

Math Performance Recording Chart

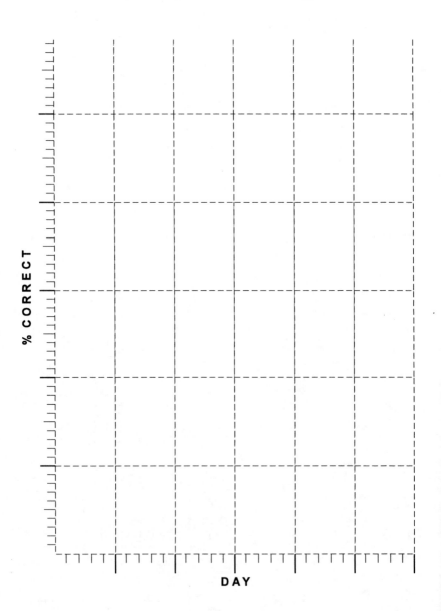

Other Sopris Publications of Interest . . .

50 Simple Ways To Make Teaching More Fun

If you're a teacher you gotta have this book!

Bob Algozzine

In this useful little book, written for both beginning and experienced teachers, the author provides suggestions and practical tips that can be used right away without special preparation or materials. **You gotta have this book** if you are preparing to teach. It is full of down-to-earth know-how and practical hints they don't provide in college. Stuff like how to use BINGO and other games to help students practice any content or how to reduce bothersome behavior with a simple recording system.

You gotta have this book if you are already teaching. It is full of practical information and sample worksheets you search for in teacher workshops. Stuff like how to use PALINDROMES to help students practice math or how to encourage students' creative thinking

Humorous examples and real-life stories illustrate these simple ways to make teaching fun.

Strategies and Tactics for Effective Instruction (STEI)

Arm yourself with alternatives for teaching the "tough-to-teach"

Bob Algozzine and James E. Ysseldyke

Effective teaching is a complex process. Research has shown that there are effective ways to plan, manage, deliver, and evaluate instruction. Yet, tactics that work with some students often do not work with others. Teachers will find *Strategies and Tactics for Effective Instruction (STEI)* a treasure chest of information on teaching tactics that work.

STEI is a flexible instructional improvement tool that can be used for individual student interventions, instructional consultation, prereferral intervention, as a teacher training tool, and as a support team resource (SST, TAT, etc.). It can be used not only by classroom teachers but also related service personnel, such as school psychologists, resource teachers, and instructional consultants.

● Training Available

The Tough Kid Book

Practical Classroom Management Strategies

Ginger Rhode, William R. Jenson, and H. Kenton Reavis

Do you hate going to work on Mondays because of a small number of students who make your teaching life miserable? Do these students make you doubt your effectiveness, as well as wonder why you ever went into education? Do these "tough kids" argue with you continuously, throw tantrums, lack motivation, appear socially immature, and ruin the learning environment for other students? If you answered "yes" to any of these questions and want **practical solutions**, this book is for you.

If you are preparing to teach (and thus work with tough kids), this book will be a survival manual for your first years of teaching. If you are a practicing teacher, this is a resource they should have used when you were in college. *The Tough Kid Book* is a resource for both regular and special education teachers. The research-validated solutions included in this book are designed to maximally reduce disruptive behavior in tough kids without big investments on the teacher's part in terms of time, money, and emotion. The solutions also provide tough kids with behavioral, academic, and social survival skills. This publication contains a wealth of ready-to-use strategies and identifies other commercially available, practical resources for teachers who want even more in-depth assistance.

Use *The Tough Kid Book* to make the classroom a pleasant, productive environment for you and your students. Learn to enjoy teaching and Monday mornings again—turn tough kids into **great kids**!

● Training Available

For Further Information

Call: (800) 547-6747   or   **Visit our Website:** www.sopriswest.com